T0148830

French Canadians in Michigan

DISCOVERING THE PEOPLES OF MICHIGAN
Arthur W. Helweg and Linwood H. Cousins, Series Editors

Ethnicity in Michigan: Issues and People
Jack Glazier, Arthur W. Helweg

French Canadians in Michigan
John P. DuLong

African Americans in Michigan
Lewis Walker, Benjamin C. Wilson, Linwood H. Cousins

Albanians in Michigan
Frances Trix

Discovering the Peoples of Michigan is a series of publications examining the state's rich multicultural heritage. The series makes available an interesting, affordable, and varied collection of books that enables students and lay readers to explore Michigan's ethnic dynamics. A knowledge of the state's rapidly changing multicultural history has far-reaching implications for human relations, education, public policy, and planning. We believe that Discovering the Peoples of Michigan will enhance understanding of the unique contributions that diverse and often unrecognized communities have made to Michigan's history and culture.

French Canadians in Michigan

John P. DuLong

Michigan State University Press

East Lansing

⊚ The paper used in this publication meets the minimum requirements
of ANSI/NISO Z39.48-1992 (R 1997) (Permanence of Paper)

Michigan State University Press
East Lansing, Michigan 48823-5202
Printed and bound in the United States of America

07 06 05 04 03 02 01   1 2 3 4 5 6 7

LIBRARY OF CONGRESS CATALOGING-IN-PUBLICATION DATA
DuLong, John P.
French Canadians in Michigan / John DuLong.
p. cm. — (Discovering the peoples of Michigan)
Includes bibliographical references and index.
ISBN 0-87013-582-1 (alk. paper)
1. French-Canadians—Michigan—History. 2. Michigan—Ethnic relations.
3. Michigan—History. 4. Michigan—Emigration and immigration—History.
5. Québec (Province)—Emigration and immigration—History. I. Title. II. Series.
F575.F85 D85 2001
977.4'004114—dc21
2001000396

Discovering the People of Michigan. The editors wish
to thank the Kellogg Foundation for their generous support.

Cover design by Ariana Grabec-Dingman
Book design by Sharp Designs, Inc.

COVER PHOTO: Lumberjack lunch break, Saginaw River Valley.
James Cook Mills, History of Saginaw County, 2 vols. (Saginaw,
Mich.: Seeman & Peters, 1918) 1:401.

Visit Michigan State University Press on the World Wide Web at:
www.msupress.msu.edu

To Joseph Leo DuLong and Catherine Olive Stanton,
my parents and my connection to Quebec and Acadia.

ACKNOWLEDGMENTS

I would like to thank Charles Hyde, Department of History, Wayne State University, and Jean Lamarre, Department of History, Royal Military College of Canada, for critically reading an earlier draft of this manuscript. I have also benefited from the insightful assistance of Keith R. Widder, Senior Editor, Michigan State University Press.

SERIES ACKNOWLEDGMENTS

Discovering the Peoples of Michigan is a series of publications that resulted from the cooperation and effort of many individuals. The people recognized here are not a complete representation, for the list of contributors is too numerous to mention. However, credit must be given to Jeffrey Bonevich, who worked tirelessly with me on contacting people as well as researching and organizing material. He read and reread, checked and rechecked, and continually kept in contact with contributors.

The initial idea for this project came from Mary Erwin, but I must thank Fred Bohm, director of the Michigan State University Press, for seeing the need for this project, for giving it his strong support, and for making publication possible. Also, the tireless efforts of Keith Widder and Elizabeth Demers, senior editors at Michigan State University Press, were vital in bringing DPOM to fruition. Keith put his heart and soul into this series, and his dedication was instrumental in its success.

Otto Feinstein and Germaine Strobel of the Michigan Ethnic Heritage Studies Center patiently and willingly provided names for contributors and constantly gave this project their tireless support.

My late wife, Usha Mehta Helweg, was the initial editor. She meticulously went over manuscripts. Her suggestions and advice were crucial. Initial typing, editing, and formatting were also done by Majda Seuss, Priya Helweg, and Carol Nickolai.

Many of the maps were drawn by Fritz Seegers while the graphics showing ethnic residential patterns in Michigan were done by the Geographical Information Center (GIS) at Western Michigan University under the directorship of David Dickason. Ellen R. White contributed additional maps.

Russell Magnaghi must also be given special recognition for his willingness to do much more than be a contributor. He provided author contacts as well as information to the series' writers. Other authors and organizations provided comments on other aspects of the work. There are many people that were interviewed by the various authors who will remain anonymous. However, they have enabled the story of their group to be told. Unfortunately, their names are not available, but we are grateful for their cooperation.

Most of all, this work is a tribute to the writers who patiently gave their time to write and share their research findings. Their contributions are noted and appreciated. To them goes most of the gratitude.

ARTHUR W. HELWEG, *Series Co-editor*

Contents

Introduction

The population of Michigan originated with numerous Native American tribes who had lived here for centuries. Over the last four hundred years at least seventy-five ethnic groups coming from 150 countries have given the state one of the most ethnically diverse populations in the United States. Discovering the Peoples of Michigan is a series of publications that chronicles the experiences of Michigan's diverse people providing an economical, flexible, and current portrayal on a variety of topics for readers who want to learn about and/or become involved in the affairs of a particular ethnic community. It is hoped that volumes in this series will help readers to understand better and to deal with the rapid ethnic diversification that is taking place in Michigan.

Discovering the Peoples of Michigan provides a comprehensive ethnographic portrait of Michigan's ethnic groups to help people understand ethnic and multicultural issues affecting Michigan. To do this, we assembled experts to write volumes containing information about each group's place of origin, their ongoing relationship with their homeland, a brief history of their presence in Michigan, and their contributions to their adopted state set within a national and global context.

In 1941, the contributors to *Michigan: A Guide to the Wolverine State* wrestled with the concept of Michigan's identity. The writers focused on the production of copper, lumber, and automobiles, but they said little about people. Michigan's identity is not in the production of goods; it is in its human resources. Michigan's people, representing many cultural heritages, have shaped the state's identity, meaning, and purpose. Thus, it is fitting that the story of the French Canadians be told since they were the first Europeans to enter the Great Lakes region and Michigan. They were not only crucial in laying the foundation for the development of Michigan's culture and economy, but they illustrate the process of ethnogenesis—they evolved into a community that is neither French nor Canadian, yet they have tenaciously held on to those cultural traits that they deem important. Their fascinating story follows.

Arthur W. Helweg
Linwood H. Cousins

French Canadians in Michigan

John P. DuLong

rench Canadians share a common history, religion, culture, and
location. Their settlements were primarily along the St. Lawrence
River and in the scattered outposts of the former French territories
in North America. They are chiefly French-speaking Catholics with ties
to the Canadian province of Quebec. Due to their French language and
Canadian origin, scholars often lump them hastily and haphazardly
with other Americans of French ancestry or with Canadians. Ironically,
French Canadians are no longer French nor do they have an unshak-
able Canadian identity.

The French Canadians are the descendants of the original explorers
and settlers who came to Canada. Canada was then part of New France,
which eventually stretched from Acadia in the Canadian Maritimes to
the Rocky Mountains and from Hudson's Bay to Louisiana. Most of
these people came from Paris (Ile-de-France) or the coastal provinces
of northern and western France, mainly Normandy, Brittany, Poitou,
and Aunis. But French Canadians also have Walloon, Swiss, Basque,
Portuguese, Spanish, Irish, Scottish, English, German, and Italian fore-
bears, as well as English and Dutch captives from New England and
New Netherland in their ancestry. Furthermore, many of them, especially in the Midwest, have some Indian ancestry.

1

Their diverse background, combined with the adaptations required for life on the frontier, resulted in a unique cultural framework. Their Canadian environment meant living adjacent to the free-spirited Indians, surviving incredibly harsh winters compared to Europe, and working as fur traders released from the restraints of confining "civilization." These factors encouraged the rapid development of a unique character in a single generation, much to the chagrin of the French colonial administrators. According to W. J. Eccles:

> The royal officials continually complained that the Canadians always pleased themselves and paid little attention to directives that did not suit their fancy. Visitors to the colony also commented on the proclivity, that the Canadians could be led but not driven.[1]

This streak of independence can be observed in the insistence of French Canadians to be called *habitants* and not peasants like their counterparts in France. They arose from a colonial experience and shared more similarities with Americans and Mexicans than with the French. It is impossible to pinpoint the moment at which a colonial people becomes a nation. However, as Guy Frégault suggests, a distinctive French Canadian identity emerged early on, separate from that of French nationals. This national character was well established by the time Canada was conquered.[2]

The French Canadians should not be confused with Canadians. During the French colonial period they were once proudly known as *Canadiens*. Eventually, this label was applied to all residents of Canada whether of English, Irish, Scottish, German, Ukrainian, or French ancestry. The French Canadians have a separate cultural history from the rest of Canada and they consciously preserve it. As today's separatist movement in Quebec demonstrates, not all French Canadians consider themselves Canadians. The modernization of Quebec in the 1960s, known as the "quiet revolution," raised the social consciousness of the people. As a result of these changes, the French Canadians of Quebec have come to refer to themselves as *Quebecois*. The French Canadians in Michigan do not call themselves Quebecois, because most of them descend from emigrants who left Quebec before the social changes of the 1960s and the subsequent separatist movement. Michigan's French Canadians do not share the same ethnic label with their cousins in Quebec, nor have they embraced the separatist cause. Still, they do share the sentiment that they are part of a separate nationality from anglophone Canadians.

The leaders of French Canadian communities in the United States popularized the term Franco-American near the turn of the twentieth century. These are all people of French ancestry living in the United States.[3] According to the 1970 census, French Canadians compose the single largest block of Franco-Americans in the United States. Canadians make up approximately 49% of the foreign-born French speakers and 68% of the second-generation French speakers in the United States.[4] Likewise, the French Canadians probably make up well over half of the Franco-Americans in Michigan. The French Canadians of the New England states still frequently use the term Franco-American, but its use has gradually died out in the Midwest.

French Canadians came to Michigan in two separate waves of immigration. The first happened between 1660 and 1796 and the second occurred between 1840 and 1930. Each movement had different patterns of migration, settlement, work, and community life, and faced different challenges. There was little interaction between these two groups of immigrants except in the Detroit area. This historical pattern makes it necessary to divide this essay into two parts separated by a section devoted to the years between the French colonial period and the American industrial period. A brief discussion of French Canadians today concludes the essay.

French Canadians during the Colonial Period

The French and French Canadians were the first European people to explore and settle in Michigan. Although some French Canadians came to Michigan to assist the missionaries, most came to participate in the fur trade, Michigan's first industry. The French Canadians initially traveled through Michigan as *voyageurs* paddling canoes laden with fur pelts, or they came to live as unlicensed traders (*coureurs des bois*) among the Indians. It was the French Canadians who guided,

Locations of French Canadian Communities in Michigan

Figure 1. Locations of French Canadian Communities in Michigan: The French Canadians in the industrial period settled in areas quite different from those where their colonial counterparts lived.

transported, and protected the famous French missionaries and explorers. It was they who built the missions and the forts under the direction of French leaders. Within a short time the French Canadians negotiated with the Indians, administered outposts, and settled on the land.

The first European settlements in Michigan were either missions or military posts that became centers of fur trade activity. The Jesuits built missions at L'Anse on Keweenaw Bay (1660), Sault Ste. Marie (1668), and St. Ignace (1671) to serve the local tribes.[5] René-Robert Cavelier de La Salle, the famous explorer, established the short-lived Fort Miami near present-day St. Joseph in 1679, and the Jesuits founded a mission in this area around 1688. In 1691, the French built Fort St. Joseph at the present site of Niles. Small communities of mostly seasonal French Canadian residents, attached to the fur trade, grew around these outposts. The Jesuit missionaries would have preferred that the French Canadians did not live among the Indians as the *habitants* often provided less than ideal examples of Christian living and often adopted the more comfortable ways of the Indians. Over time, some French Canadians who regularly worked in the Michigan fur trade settled down with Indian wives or brought wives from Quebec.

The two most important French Canadian communities during colonial times were Detroit and Michilimackinac. The Gascon scoundrel known to popular history as Antoine de Lamothe Cadillac was instrumental in founding Detroit.[6] He persuaded Louis XIV, king of France, to move the main French fort at St. Ignace from the Straits of Mackinac to the narrows (*d'étroit*) between Lake St. Clair and Lake Erie. This was a calculated move from which he expected to profit handsomely. It was also in direct opposition to the business interests of the merchants in Montreal. Cadillac claimed that from Detroit he could prevent Indians from trading illegally with the British, who were making inroads into the region. A French presence at Detroit, he promised, would diminish the growing importance of the British in the Great Lakes region. His scheme called for the settlement of French Canadians and Indians who would meld together and become loyal subjects of His Most Christian Majesty. Cadillac established Detroit on 24 July 1701 as Fort Pontchartrain, named after the Minister of Marine who controlled the colonies and who was his protector.

Although Cadillac was initially successful at attracting the Ottawas, Potawatomis, and Wyandottes (also known as Hurons) to Detroit, his dream of a Gallic-Indian melting pot failed to materialized. There were never enough French and French Canadians to create the kind of community envisioned by Cadillac. Furthermore, he was a failure as governor. He discouraged many French Canadians from settling at Detroit because of his tyrannical rule. The village did not become desirable to settlers until Cadillac and his cronies were removed and competent administrators replaced them in 1729.[7]

The remoteness of Detroit also contributed to its slow growth. According to Almon Parkins: "Detroit was in many respects a premature settlement. It was not the logical outgrowth of a migrating people as were all later American settlements in the interior."[8] The government of New France had enough problems populating the St. Lawrence River valley. It ignored far-off Detroit as long as it served its purpose to protect French interests in the region.

People traveling from Quebec to Detroit and the other Michigan posts during the seventeenth and early eighteenth centuries faced severe challenges. Starting at Montreal one journeyed northwest by going up the Ottawa River, turning on to the Mattawa River, then across to Lake Nipissing, to the French River, and on into Georgian Bay. From there the Great Lakes opened west to Michilimackinac and Lake Michigan, northwest to Sault Ste. Marie and Lake Superior, and south to Detroit through Lake Huron. This was a difficult route with over thirty portages. The Iroquois living in upstate New York, who were allies of the Dutch and British, interfered with French traffic throughout most of the seventeenth century. The 1701 peace with the Iroquois allowed most French Canadians to follow a more southerly route up the St. Lawrence River and westward through Lakes Ontario and Erie to Detroit. After the Seven Years' War (French and Indian War), the British built large sailing vessels to move people and goods across Lake Erie and up Lake Huron.

Despite the hostility of the Iroquois, relations with the Indians cannot be blamed for the slow growth of Detroit. With one other notable exception, the French Canadians in Detroit interacted cordially with thousands of neighboring Indians. This was undoubtedly due to the crucial role played by the Indians in the fur trade. In 1712, however, the French at Detroit, fearing an assault by the Foxes, attacked the nearby Fox village and drove the survivors to Wisconsin.[9]

French desires to defeat the Foxes living west of Lake Michigan led to the reestablishment of a fort and community at the Straits of Mackinac. Although the Jesuits maintained their mission on the north side of the straits at St. Ignace, the French military abandoned the fort there in 1698. By 1715, the French had constructed a fort on the south side of the straits near the relocated Jesuit mission and Ottawa village. The French used Fort Michilimackinac as their base in the war against the Foxes who had fled to the Green Bay–Lake Winnebago area in eastern Wisconsin, where they blockaded the Fox-Wisconsin waterway. The French fought against the Foxes for decades.

The straits rapidly resumed its role as the center of the western Great Lakes fur trade, and Michilimackinac became a strategic point on the map of New France. Every summer canoe brigades arrived from Montréal to rendezvous with trappers and Indians at the small settlement. The population of the village swelled, but in winter it dropped to a handful of residents. Strictly tied to the fur trade, the French Canadian settlers depended on the Indians not only for furs but also for fish, meat, corn, and spouses.

Although the French government established settlements in Michigan, French Canadians populated and eventually administered them. In 1710, 59% of the thirty-four Detroit households were French Canadian as opposed to native-born French.[10] By 1750 the population of Detroit was 483 inhabitants plus transient voyageurs, Indians, and soldiers. These soldiers were of the *Compagnies franches de la Marine*, also known as *Troupes de la Marine*, and many of them settled at Detroit when they retired from service.[11] Except for these soldiers, most of whom were born in France, Detroit residents were mostly French Canadian. By 1778 the population stood at 2,144.[12] Only a handful of Detroit residents were British or American; the vast majority were French Canadian. Most of this growth was due to natural increase as well as a French government-sponsored settlement plan launched in 1749 that continued until 1752.

This mid-eighteenth-century colonizing effort was a reaction to the struggle with the British over control of the Ohio River valley. In an attempt to populate Detroit with farmers rather than transient fur traders, the governor of New France offered new settlers land, animals, and tools, and he forbade them to engage in the fur trade. Of the twenty-seven known settlers who took advantage of this offer, 63% were French Canadians.[13] Throughout the French period the majority of the Michigan settlers came from the Montreal area.

Over time, the administration of Michigan settlements became less French and more French Canadian. Of the eighteen known commanders at Detroit, half were French and the rest French Canadian. Before 1727 all six commanders were Frenchmen, but of the twelve commanders

French Canadians at Michilimackinac

There are ten French families in the fort among whom three are of mixed blood; although this piece of land is quite barren they could nevertheless give themselves some of the comforts of life if they were more laborious, for the soil produces as good peas as may be seen, beans also grow very well, all root crops in general would do as well; but it would cost them too much effort to procure these good things for themselves. They prefer strolling around the fort's parade ground, from morn till night, with a pipe in their mouth and a tobacco pouch on their left arm, rather than take the least pain to make life more comfortable. . . . They only take the trouble of going to the edge of the lake, as if going to the market, to get their supplies of corn and fish when the Indians bring some. They prefer living on corn, fish, and deer or moose grease. . . . They make use of Maple water which they let turn sour, and of rather clear bear oil of the same color and taste as lard when it is in the process of cooling down. . . . To put it briefly, they are content as long as they have their corn and grease to live on all year round, which makes me think that for as long as there will be one single pelt to be had in these countries they will never engage in any other business. The traders of this place, who all turned merchants after having made three or four trips as *engagés*, and who must be farmers since they all come from rural areas, would feel dishonored if they cultivated the soil.

—*Observations of Michel Chartier de Lotbinière in 1749.*[42]

after 1727, nine were French Canadian. A similar pattern can be found at Michilimackinac where the first two commanders were French and the other eleven were French Canadian.[14]

While Michilimackinac remained exclusively a fur trading post, Detroit became the most developed settlement west of Montreal. By the end of the French period, the farms of the French Canadians stretched out on both sides of the Detroit River. These ribbon farms had a narrow frontage on the river and a depth that stretch back into the wilderness. The houses were built on the river's edge and because of their proximity to one another they gave the impression of one long village.

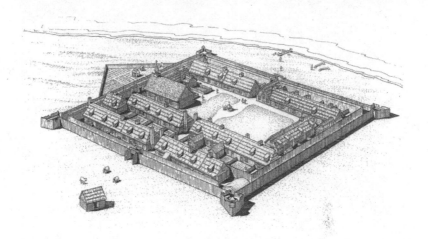

Figure 2. Fort Michilimackinac as it probably looked in 1749 based on Lotbinière's drawing. Drawn by Victor Hogg. Taken from Marie Gérin-Lajoie, trans. and ed., Fort Michilimackinac in 1749: Lotbinière's Plan and Description, Mackinac History, *vol. 2, leaflet no. 5 (Mackinac Island: Mackinac Island State Park Commission, 1976), 3–4. Courtesy of the Mackinac State Historic Parks, Michigan.*

Because the French Canadian settlers at Detroit could not resist the fur trade, they became known as indifferent farmers. Even farmers who came in 1749 found it difficult to avoid participating in the fur trade economy. They sold the little surplus that they grew in their gardens to local fur traders. Yet, during the crucial war years of the 1750s, when a market developed, they produced a surplus in their fields that fed the French forces operating in the Ohio country. French Canadian agriculturists also had planted many fruit trees, and Detroit was well known for its apple and pear orchards.

The inhabitants of Detroit supported several craftsmen including a mason, a carpenter, a baker, a butcher, and two blacksmiths. The area had two sawmills run by water, and four gristmills, two of these being windmills. The village even boasted a notary, Robert Navarre.

Social life in Detroit came to resemble that in Quebec. The parish of Ste. Anne served as the center of social activity on Sunday and throughout the week. The French Canadians celebrated a mild form of Mardi

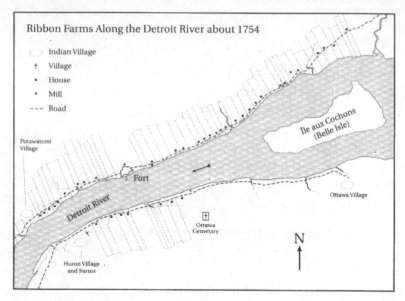

Figure 3. Detroit River around 1754: The pattern of ribbon farms can be clearly seen on this map. Adapted from "Plan topgraphique du Détroit," by Gal. Collot, 1796, based on the 1754 map of Chaussegros de Léry. Burton Historical Collection, Detroit Public Library.

Gras before Lent; Christmas was primarily a religious feast day. On New Year's Day, their most important holiday, people went from house to house wishing one another well. Beyond their parish-centered preoccupations, the men enjoyed playing fierce games of lacrosse with their Indian neighbors. They also raced their sleds on the frozen river in winter and their two-wheeled *calèches* on dusty paths in the summer for the enjoyment of their families and friends. Women hosted each other as they sewed or drank warm beverages on cold winter days.

There was little in the way of education and few French Canadians could read. Nevertheless, they had a rich folklore with many entertaining stories and songs.[15] Their life centered around their families, their parish, their traditions from Quebec and France, and their interactions with the Indians in the fur trade. In sum, at the end of the French period, Detroit had become a small Canadian parish tied to the fur trade for its survival. Cadillac's plans for Detroit succeeded in spite of his acrimonious behavior.

The Transition Period

With the British conquest of Canada in 1760, the political realities changed for the French Canadians in Michigan, but their dependency on the fur trade economy remained. The greatest change they noticed was the loss of control in the fur trade. The French Canadians throughout British North America began to work for English and Scottish businessmen rather than French or French Canadian merchants. There were fewer opportunities for social mobility.

Three separate occasions tested the loyalty of the French Canadians to the British: Pontiac's Uprising in 1763, the American Revolution and its aftermath from 1775 to 1796, and the War of 1812. In all three instances most French Canadians remained neutral. Those who became active usually backed the interests of the British Crown, yet a few could be found in the opposition. Each war presented the French Canadian community with difficult choices.

The best example of the perplexing alternatives the French Canadians faced is the American Revolution. On the one hand, there were several factors favoring the cause of the Crown: (1) the British were in control of the fur trade; (2) the Quebec Act protected the interests of French Canadians and the Catholic religion; (3) their Indian neighbors were supporting the British by raiding the American frontier settlements and some French Canadian militiamen frequently accompanied them; (4) the British had defeated the 1775 American invasion of Canada; and (5) many Americans held strong anti-Catholic feelings. On the other hand, the cause of the American rebels appealed to French Canadians for several reasons: (1) resentment against the British as conquerors; (2) many of the Michigan French Canadians' cousins in the Illinois country had supported the American cause; and (3) the 1778 alliance between France and the Americans. Many Michigan French Canadians reluctantly supported the British from the beginning of the American Revolution through 1796 when the Crown transferred Detroit to the United States. They all awaited the outcome of what was essentially for them a struggle between *les anglais et les bostonnais*.

War disrupted the lives of French Canadians. Great Britain ceded their claims to Indian lands in the United States, without conferring with either Indian or French Canadian inhabitants. The French Canadians' ties with their St. Lawrence valley homeland were seriously weakened. The lack of written records left by French Canadians (most of whom were illiterate) makes it difficult to determine their opinions relative to their changing world. The prejudiced views of British officials, never pleased with less than total support by the French Canadians, are also difficult to interpret. In fact, from 1760 to 1774 some British administrators actually discussed the forced removal of the frontier French Canadians to Quebec.[16] Nevertheless, one pattern that emerges is that most French Canadians continued to work in the fur trade. They did nothing that jeopardized their livelihood. Consequently, most of them remained neutral or professed loyalty to British interests and did not oppose their employers.

Another consequence of these wars was the American belief that the French Canadians assisted the Indians in committing such atrocities as the Ojibwa attack on Fort Michilimackinac during Pontiac's Uprising, the raids on frontier settlements during the American Revolution, and the massacre following the battle of the River Raisin during the War of 1812. These remembrances colored the point of view of Americans that French Canadians were: ". . . of unstable loyalties, of undependable veracity, ultra-conservative and a limiting block to progressive improvement."[17]

By the time the Americans took control of Michigan, the distribution of French Canadians had changed. Detroit itself had become a British village with most of the French Canadians living on nearby farms. Around 1785, François Navarre founded Frenchtown on the banks of the River Raisin about thirty-four miles south of Detroit. This became the village of Monroe and was the third most important French Canadian settlement in Michigan. Monroe County still has the largest number of French Canadian descendants from the first wave of immigration. Although the French language is no longer spoken in Monroe, some customs are still practiced. In particular, muskrat, a French Canadian delicacy, is still served in some Monroe homes. When the Americans came to Detroit, more French Canadians fled. They preferred to live in Monroe or to cross the Detroit River to a community that became Windsor, Ontario. When the British established Fort Malden at

Figure 4. The Lasselle farm on the River Raisin, Monroe, Michigan: This painting by Charles Lanman shows a typical example of a French Canadian house with a steep roof and dormers that could once be found all along the Detroit River. Private collection. Photo courtesy of the Monroe County Historical Commission.

Amherstburg in 1796, some French Canadian families, especially those associated with the British Indian Department, moved to this location. Eventually, many of the French Canadians migrated north of Windsor to the Belle River area on the south shore of Lake St. Clair. Although separated by a political border, many of the French Canadian families in Amherstburg and Belle River can claim, along with people from Monroe, descent from the same early Detroit settlers.

When the United States established a government in Michigan in 1796, the French Canadians made up roughly eighty percent of the European-American population.[18] They still remained in the majority in 1820 when they numbered more than six thousand out of about nine thousand residents.[19] The flood of Yankees from the northeast states, in part due to the opening of the Erie canal in 1825, rapidly submerged them. At the time of statehood in 1837, they were already a minority. Although French Canadians usually remained in the political

Métis

In French, the word *métis* means "one of mixed blood," [*Merriam-Webster's Collegiate Dictionary*, 10th ed. (Springfield, Mass.: Merriam-Webster, Inc. 1999), 732]. It came to be applied to people of mixed French and Indian ancestry. Compared to French Canadians in Quebec, many more French Canadians in Michigan have an Indian heritage. Typically, a French Canadian man took an Indian woman as his wife, more often married by tribal custom than a French religious ceremony. The marriage was often made to facilitate trade relationships. Both Métis male and female offspring played important roles as cultural brokers in the fur trade. Men often participated in military affairs as leaders of war parties or in militias, and some served as interpreters for the French and later the British. Women connected their Indian kin to the fur-trading enterprises of their French Canadian and Métis husbands. Over the decades the Métis in Michigan have blended in with either their Indian families or in French Canadian communities. There is no strong, independent ethnic identity of Métis in Michigan like there is among the Métis of Manitoba, Saskatchewan, and Alberta in the Canadian West. Nevertheless, many Michigan French Canadians can proudly claim blood ties with Michigan Indians.

Magdelaine Laframboise and Charles-Michel Mouet de Langlade were two of Michigan's most prominent Métis who spent much of their lives at Mackinac. Both had French Canadian fathers, who traded furs, and mothers who came from influential Ottawa families.[44]

background, they might have played an important role in the political life of the new state. In 1823, the support of French Canadians elected the French priest Father Gabriel Richard as the non-voting delegate from Michigan Territory to serve in Congress. Richard was the first priest to be seated by Congress. The French Canadians, however, never developed their political potential, and the election of Father Richard was their last show of strength in Michigan.

As the fur trade declined in importance after the 1820s, the French Canadians became more geographically dispersed and outnumbered and more isolated from their Canadian homeland. Consequently, the

Michigan French Canadians began to assimilate slowly into the American way of life. If not for the sudden rush of the second wave of immigration, the French Canadians would have blended almost completely into the social background.

Although many French Canadians are mentioned in the history books, few who were permanently settled or raised in Michigan became affluent. The most interesting exception is Joseph Campau, a businessman, who was once one of the wealthiest citizens of Detroit. Now all that remains of his fame is a street named after him in Detroit. One example of the persistence of the French Canadians legacy, however, is that many of Detroit's most prominent contemporary families descend through maternal lines from the earlier French Canadian settlers.[20]

Many more humble residents of Michigan and the Midwest can trace their heritage back to the early French Canadian migrants. They left behind many family surnames including Beaubien, Cadotte, Campau, Drouillard, Langlade, Navarre, Parent, Réaume, and Tremblay. They also had an impact on the place names of Michigan, including Au Sable, Detroit, Grand Traverse Bay, Grosse Point, Grosse Isle, and Presque Isle. Despite Michigan's French and French Canadian history, it lacks a Gallic tradition like the one in Louisiana. As George Fuller observed, this may be due to the Detroit fire of 1805 that completely destroyed any possibility of preserving a "French Quarter."[21] After the fire, the French Canadians' impact on the cultural ambience of Detroit waned.

French Canadians During the Industrial Period

The second wave of French Canadian migration to the United States started as a trickle soon after the unsuccessful 1837-1838 Patriots' Rebellion in Canada. French Canadian immigration slowly built until the time of the Civil War when many returned to Canada to avoid the draft. After the draft ended in 1865, the flood gates opened and many French Canadians entered New England, New York, and Michigan. The peak of French Canadian migration was from 1880 to 1890, and it slowly tapered off until it dropped dramatically after the Great Depression of the 1930s.[22]

The increasing inability of French Canadian farmers to make a living became the leading cause of their migration out of Quebec. Although lumbering and shipbuilding became important sources of employment in Canada, these industries did not provide enough year-round jobs in Quebec. Other industrial opportunities were also too limited to support the growing number of surplus farm laborers. In the nineteenth century, Quebec agriculture was in a dismal condition as farming shifted from crops to diarying, which required fewer laborers than staple crop production. In addition, the inefficient cultivation techniques that the French Canadians employed earlier had damaged much of the land's productivity. French Canadian farm families carried a heavy debt load as they worked the depleted soil. Families also divided the patrimony with each succeeding generation, which meant smaller and less profitable holdings. In addition, the Canadian government was hesitant to release virgin land for families to start new farms. As the available productive land was decreasing, the population was increasing due to sustained high levels of fertility among the French Canadians.[23]

While Quebec industrialized at an agonizingly slow pace, across the border in New England and New York there were abundant jobs in the textile mills and the timber industry. Railroad lines connecting Quebec with these neighboring states made emigration easy. American employers were eager to hire French Canadians because they viewed them as submissive employees unlikely to become involved in labor agitation. Opportunities for work also opened up in the Midwest, first in lumbering and then in mining.

Many French Canadians in Quebec had grown accustomed to a lifestyle that accommodated seasonal work as lumberjacks in the winter and farming throughout the rest of the year. As lumbering became more important in Maine, New York, and Pennsylvania, French Canadians sought employment there, and many came to Michigan as the timber industry moved from the northeastern states to the white pine forests of the upper Midwest. About 75% of Canadian immigrants going to Michigan were lumberjacks.[24] Many of these men were initially transient, coming to work in logging during the winter and spring and returning to Quebec in the off season.

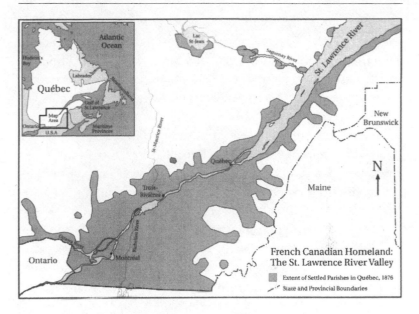

Figure 5. Origins of French Canadians in Quebec.

The Catholic hierarchy in Quebec as well as lay French Canadian leaders discouraged migration to New England and New York preferring the American Midwest or the Canadian West. According to Mason Wade: "The Quebec clergy had opposed the migration to New England from the start, favoring agricultural pioneering in Quebec or the U.S. Midwest instead, on the ground that, as day laborers in cities and factory towns, the emigrants lost everything that Canadians held dearest: religion, language, and nationality."[25] New England was, after all, a hostile urban and industrial environment that was overwhelmingly Protestant. The theory among the French Canadian elite was that their emigrants should move into the former French territories developed by the fur trade and work in lumbering and farming. This would make them more likely to maintain their language, culture, and religion. Many French Canadian immigrants to Michigan, who first settled in New England or New York, came because their leaders encouraged them to move to the Midwest. It is ironic that now, a century later, the French Canadian communities in New England have done a far better job of preserving their language and culture than those in the Midwest.

Preliminary evidence from this author's genealogical research shows that the Montreal region was a source of much immigration to Michigan. The area northwest of Montreal along the Ottawa River contributed many workers from its wood products industry. In contrast, many of the immigrants to New England came from south of the St. Lawrence River, especially from counties near the United States.[26] In both cases, most people were from rural areas. Also, some French Canadian families emigrating to Michigan had first lived in New England or New York. Others had resided for a while in the Kankakee-Bourbonnais area of Illinois or the Green Bay-Manitowoc area of Wisconsin before drifting to Michigan.

The newly arriving French Canadians first settled in places supported by lumbering or mining.[27] Many bachelors came to Michigan to work as lumberjacks in the Saginaw River valley. Others took up residence with their families in the lumber mill towns of Saginaw and Bay Counties. Eventually, sawmill towns along the coasts of Lakes Michigan and Huron drew many French Canadians. The iron and copper mining ranges in Marquette and Houghton Counties, with their incessant demands for labor, also attracted French Canadians. Many French Canadians from Essex County, Ontario (descendants of the first wave settlers in Detroit), as well as immigrants directly from Quebec, moved to Wayne County as economic opportunities grew there. Lastly, some French Canadians living along the shorelines of Lakes Huron and Michigan took up commercial fishing.

Coming from a rural lifestyle that emphasized working outside in the woods or on farms, few French Canadians moved into urban settings or worked in factories during the nineteenth century. During winter they lived in lumber camps, cut down trees, and worked in sawmills throughout the state. In spring, lumberjacks joined the dangerous river drives to bring pine logs to sawmills. As an area was cleared out, the younger and more adventurous French Canadians moved further north or west in search of other timber regions to harvest. Older married men often settled down on farms in the cleared out areas to raise their families. Some took up carpentry.

In the iron and copper mining regions of the Upper Peninsula, French Canadians worked outdoors rather than inside the mines. They

Figure 6. Lumberjack lunch break somewhere in the Saginaw River valley: Rugged outdoor work with hearty meals thrown in appealed to many French Canadians. Taken from James Cook Mills, History of Saginaw County, (Saginaw, Mich.: Seemann & Peters, 1918), 1:401.

found jobs as mine surface workers, carpenters, lumberjacks, or teamsters. Many of them worked in the stamp mills that crushed the rock to separate the ore. Others labored in smelters, processing copper ore into ingots. Although some of the French Canadians living in the mining regions abandoned working for companies to take up farming, they were less successful than their counterparts in the Lower Peninsula where the soil and climate were better suited to farming.

Some men became tradesmen or professionals serving their local community. They opened general stores, barber shops, livery stables, and saloons to provide services to their compatriots. Like other ethnic groups, they tended to live together in neighborhoods or sections of larger towns. These places were often referred to as "Little Canada" or "Frenchtown." In the mining country they often lived in company towns where employers provided housing, a store, and medical care. The French Canadians still added their own ethnic flavor to these patte.ned communities.

In regions of French Canadian settlement in Michigan, women did not have the same opportunity to work in industry as did the New

The Copper Country French Canadians

The Canadian Frenchman could not be induced to become a miner. The depths of the mine are a horror to his lively fancy and timid disposition. His forte is in the woods and his tool, *par excellence*, is an ax. In cutting cord woods, hewing timber, hauling saw [*sic*] logs, rafting and boating, etc., he is *au fait*. He avoids the great mine community and loves to dwell near the water, or in the woods, having for his companions his own people. He is clannish in this respect. He is active, patient, good natured, likes to talk, likes the violin and the dance. He spends his money freely, but is not without native shrewdness, is a good deal of a politician, and generally manages to become the owner of a small farm with a comfortable home. He is a good citizen.

—*Observations of John H. Forster writing around 1887.*[43]

England women who worked in textile mills. They reared their children and managed their households in addition to participating in the life of the local parish. Some women ran boarding houses for young single French Canadians. Over time they welcomed non-French boarders into their homes as well.

Nineteenth-century French Canadians first came to Michigan by water, but unlike their colonial counterparts they no longer rode in fragile canoes. They now booked passage on steamships that traveled through the Great Lakes. From 1855 on, many passed through the St. Mary's Falls Ship Canal joining Lake Superior to Lake Huron. Eventually, railroad service connected Michigan with Quebec making travel easier. The railroads allowed for rare trips home to visit family and friends or to make a pilgrimage to Ste. Anne-de-Beaupré, the national shrine of French Canada. Several railroads offered services between the remote French Canadian communities in the Upper Peninsula and Quebec. Despite the improved transportation system, travel to their Quebec homeland was still difficult because of the distance and cost. Compared to French Canadians in New England, those in Michigan were unable to make frequent trips to Quebec.

Although most French Canadian families contributed to the development of Michigan through manual labor, two men stand out for

Pelerinage Annuel

—A—

Ste Anne de Beaupre

✕ VIA ✕

Copper Range Railroad

Chicago et
The Grand Trunk Railway

$27.50

De tous les Points du Copper Country jusqu'a Ste Anne de Beaupre et retour.

Les Billets seront en vente tous les jours du 14 juillet au 20 inclu, avec un retour limite au 31 aout 1909.

Il sera permis d'arrêter à tous les points du Canada, et avec un petit montant additionnel on pourra visiter les fameuses chutes de Niagara.

Pour autres informations addressex-vous aux agents ou à

GEORGE WILLIAMS,
Division Passenger Agent.
Calumet, Mich.

F. R. BOLLES,
General Passenger Agent,
Houghton, Mich.

Figure 7. An advertisement for interested French Canadians to take a train to visit their home- land. French Canadians in Michigan maintained a strong interest in Quebec. As a result, special trains were often needed to handle the hundreds who returned to Quebec for visits and religious pilgrimages. C. Warren Vander Hill, Settling the Great Lakes Frontier: Immigration to Michigan, 1837–1924 (Lansing: Michigan Historical Commission, 1970), 11.

building strong businesses. Antoine E. Cartier enjoyed great success as a timber baron in Ludington. Joseph Grégoire, who employed many men in his lumber mill, became known as the father of the Lake Superior French Canadians through his efforts to encourage and help the immigrants of Houghton County.

The 1900 census reveals that the number of French Canadians relative to the state's total population had slipped dramatically. Michigan had a population of 32,483 foreign-born French Canadians and 55,314 people with both parents of French Canadian ancestry in 1900. This was approximately 3.6 percent of Michigan's population, and it shows the demographic turnover from the 1820s when they were the majority. Even if we consider the descendants of the first wave of immigrants, clearly the French Canadians were a small minority. Still the foreign-born French Canadians were the fourth largest ethnic group in Michigan. They were outnumbered by the Canadians, Germans, and English, and closely followed by the Dutch, Irish, Swedes, and Poles.[28]

Figure 8. Joseph Grégoire (or Gregory) was known as the father of Lake Superior French Canadians. He was born in St. Valentin, Quebec, in 1833. He came to Lake Linden, Michigan, when he was twenty-one years old and worked as a woodsman, then as a foreman. Soon after he became a contractor in partnership with Louis Deschamps and Joseph Normandin. They established a sawmill on Torch Lake at a site now called Gregoryville. In 1872, Grégoire became the sole owner of the sawmill. He made a point of employing French Canadian immigrants to the Copper Country. Courtesy of the State Archives of Michigan, Lansing, Michigan.

By 1950 the arrival of large numbers of Poles, Italians, and Russians had pushed the foreign-born French Canadians to the ninth largest ethnic group in the state.[29] It is interesting to note that one thing that sets apart the second wave of French Canadians from the first wave is the more complex multiethnic environment in which they lived. The early French Canadians had to interact with Indians, English, Irish, Scots, and Americans. In the industrial period French Canadians had to relate to ethnic groups from across Europe and the Middle East.

Due to the attraction of the timber and mining industries, the French Canadians tended to settle in isolated towns in rural counties. The 1900 census shows that 59% of the foreign-born French Canadians were living in just eight counties: Wayne (4,426), Houghton (3,144), Bay (2,664), Delta (2,637), Menominee (1,892), Marquette (1,765), Saginaw (1,288), and Alpena (1,197).[30] As the timber industry declined in Michigan, many French Canadians moved to Wisconsin and Minnesota to follow the logging trade. Some French Canadians who lost their jobs when mines closed went to Detroit to work in the city's growing automobile industry.

Figure 9. Distribution of Michigan's Population Claiming French Canadian Ancestry (1990).

Michigan played an important role in French Canadian settlement in the United States. Again the data from the 1900 census show that Michigan's population of foreign-born French Canadians (32,483) was behind Massachusetts (134,416) and New Hampshire (44,420) but ahead of Rhode Island (31,533), Maine (30,908), New York (27,199), and Connecticut (19,174). Furthermore, Michigan had the largest settlement of French Canadians in the Midwest when compared to Minnesota (12,063), Wisconsin (10,091), and Illinois (9,129).[31]

The Michigan French Canadians, like their counterparts in the East, were concerned with *survivance*, that is, the movement to protect and

Un Canadien Errant / The Wandering Canadian

Here is a sad French Canadian folk song that was sung by many immigrants in Michigan.

Un Canadien Errant	A wandering Canadian,
Banni de ses foyers,	Banished from his hearth,
Parcourait en pleurant	Traveled while crying
Des pays étrangers.	in a foreign land.
Parcourait en pleurant	Traveled while crying
Des pays étrangers.	in a foreign land.
Un jour, triste et pensif,	One day, sad and pensive,
Assis au bord des flots,	Seated on a river bank,
Au courant fugitif	To the fleeting current
Il adressa ces mots:	He addressed these words:
Au curant fugitif	To the fleeting current
Il adressa ces mots:	He addressed these words.
«Si tu vois mon pays,	"If you see my country,
Mon pays malheureux	My unhappy country
Va dire à mes amis	Go say to my friends
Que je me souviens d'eux.	That I remember them.
Va dire à mes amis	Go say to my friends
Que je me souviens d'eux.	That I remember them.
O jours si pleins d'appas,	O days so full with charms,
Vous êtes disparus . . .	You have disappeared . . .
Et ma patrie, hélas!	And my fatherland, alas!
Je ne la verrais plus.	I will see it no more.
Et ma patrie, hélas!	And my fatherland, alas!
Je ne la verrai plus.»	I will see it no more."

Lyrics written by Antoine Gérin-Lajoie in 1842. Translated by John P. DuLong.

foster the French language, Catholic religion, and their Canadian traditions. The French Canadians in Michigan resorted to three institutions
to maintain their culture: national parishes and parochial schools,
beneficial societies, and newspapers. By 1912 Michigan had approximately ten parishes identified as totally French and twenty-three as
partially. French, the French undoubtedly referring to French
Canadians.[32] These parishes had schools and some of them used French
as the language of instruction. Some schools imported teaching nuns
from Quebec. Although these national parishes became important centers for maintaining French Canadian ethnicity, the mostly Irish
American Catholic hierarchy initially did not favor them nor did they
always deal fairly with their French Canadian parishioners. The best
example of the glaring differences between the French Canadians and
their religious leaders can be seen in the crisis involving the parishioners of Ste. Anne's in Detroit. From the French Canadian perspective,
the bishop mishandled them and forced them to sell off adjacent property and eventually the church itself. The proceeds were divided
unequally with $100,000 used to build St. Ann for the Irish on the west
side of town and $40,000 to create St. Joachim parish in 1886 on the east
side for the French Canadians. Many French Canadians in Detroit never
forgave what they viewed as a theft of their church that dated back to
the founding of the city.[33] In addition to these perceived injustices, the
Catholic hierarchy ignored the demands of the French Canadians for
priests from their homeland.

Three factors changed the attitude of the Catholic hierarchy. First,
the controversy over the renegade Illinois priest, Father Charles Chini-
quy, who horrified Catholic officials when he became a Presbyterian
and converted some of his flock as well. Second, the defection of several other French Canadian families to Protestantism. And third, the
pressure from the flood of new Catholic immigrants from southern and
eastern Europe who wanted to follow their own ethnic traditions. After
the 1880s the Catholic hierarchy in Michigan began to tolerate ethnic
parishes and to recruit priests and nuns from Quebec.

The French Canadians, like other immigrant groups, came to rely on
mutual benefit fraternal societies that served to foster French Canadian
political, cultural, and religious interests. Among these groups were the

Figure 10. Ste. Anne's (top) and St. Joachim (bottom) Churches in Detroit. Taken from Silas Farmer, History of Detroit and Wayne County and Early Michigan: A Chronological Cyclopedia of the Past and Present *(Detroit: S. Farmer & Co., 1890), 534 and 546.*

Société de Lafayette, the Union des Canadiens-Français Catholique, the Institut Jacques Cartier, and the Association Canado-Américaine. Many French Canadians were also active in the International Order of Foresters. Several of these organizations provided life, accident, and burial insurance to their membership. The Société St-Jean-Baptiste was the largest and most important mutual benefit society in Michigan, the northeastern states, and Quebec.

The Société St-Jean-Baptiste came to Michigan in 1864 when a chapter was organized in Detroit. By the turn of the twentieth century there were chapters in Alpena, Calumet, Champion, Detroit, Hancock, Houghton, Lake Linden, Manistee, Marquette, Menominee, Muskegon, and Negaunee. The Michigan chapters had ties to the headquarters in Montreal and undoubtedly sent delegates to the various national conventions. They remained interested in Canadian affairs and sponsored protests against the execution of the Métis leader Louis Riel in Saskatchewan in 1885.

The annexation controversy, which erupted at the 1869 joint conference of French Canadian groups in Detroit to honor the memory of Napoleon Bonaparte, damaged the effectiveness of the Société St-Jean-Baptiste to represent French Canadians' interests. Médéric Lanctot, a journalist, spoke at this meeting and argued that Quebec should break away from the British and become part of the United States. He believed that French Canadians could better protect their culture, language, and religion under American auspices. Although his policy was not widely accepted, it was debated with Gallic ferocity and succeeded in fractionalizing the French Canadian community and its fraternal organizations in Michigan.

Although the Société St-Jean-Baptiste never became an effective force in politics, it played a role in the naturalization of French Canadians. At first their leaders opposed naturalization and few French Canadians bothered to become American citizens. But this attitude gradually changed after various repatriation schemes fell apart and the 1886 national St-Jean-Baptiste convention in Plattsburgh, New York, endorsed a platform of "naturalization without assimilation."[34] The Société St-Jean-Baptiste and other mutual benefit societies started to emphasize the value of naturalization. They encouraged their members

Figure 11. Tèlesphore St-Pierre, a prominent writer and historian of the French in Michigan. He was an editor for French language newspapers in Detroit, Bay City, and Lake Linden, and he wrote a history of the French Canadians in Michigan. Vander Hill, Settling the Great Lakes Frontier, 10.

to become loyal Americans, but to remain French in tradition and sentiment.

The Société fostered French Canadian traditions with its regular programs and its annual celebration of the *fête de St-Jean-Baptiste* on 24 June. French Canadians marked their national holiday with parades, picnics, speeches, and bonfires. For many French Canadians assimilation meant only waving the American flag while marching in their ethnic parade.

French Canadians used newspapers to protect their ethnicity. Between 1809 and 1919, the French Canadian communities of Michigan published thirty-three French language newspapers: Detroit (17), Bay City (7), Lake Linden (3), Marquette (2), Muskegon (2), Ludington (1), and Saginaw (1).[35] *Le Courrier du Michigan*, which became the most successful paper, started publication in Lake Linden in 1912 and moved to Detroit in 1919. Pierre-Eudore Mayrand, the paper's dedicated editor, kept it alive until 1957. Many of the others lasted only a few years and

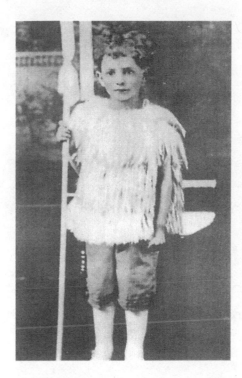

Figure 12. A French Canadian boy, Clarence Dupuis of Lake Linden, dressed as St-Jean-Baptiste (St. John the Baptist). Ritual and participation in feasts are strong tactics used to transmit culture from one generation to the next. Here the custom of dressing a boy as St-Jean-Baptiste on his feast day encourages participation. "St. Joseph Church, Lake Linden, Michigan, 1871-1971 (Lake Linden: By the Parish, 1971), 37.

some for only a few months or even weeks. Nevertheless, they showed the commitment of the French Canadian intellectuals to fostering their culture in Michigan. The papers reported happenings in the local French Canadian communities and news from Quebec. They also printed serialized French stories, biographies of famous French explorers and missionaries, and religious items. The papers took political stands. For example, they argued against the revocation of French language rights in western Canada. Prominent French Canadian intellectuals, including editors Télesphore St-Pierre and Pierre-Eudore Maynard, found newspapers to be an important forum from which to disseminate their ideas.

French Canadians Today

Despite the best efforts of many French Canadians, the French language and French Canadian customs have not been well preserved in

Tourtière Recipe

Every Christmas, like many other French Canadian families, we would have
tourtière, a special meat pie, after midnight mass. This is my grandmother's,
Exilda "Julia" (Bourbonnais) DuLong's, recipe passed down to my mother and
now my wife. Over the years, I have learned that many French Canadian families prepare it differently, for example, some add cinnamon. I offer to you my
family's recipe, which, out of loyalty, I have to consider definitive:

2 lbs. ground lean pork	2 tsp. salt
1 lb. ground lean beef	1 tsp. celery salt
2 large onions	1 tsp. pepper
1 clove garlic	1 cup. water
2½ tsp. poultry seasoning	3 medium potatoes

On top of stove add all ingredients into large stock pot or dutch oven. Cook
on medium heat for 1 hour; do not fry meat. Remove from heat and cool. Skim
off the fat from the surface. Preferably let it sit in the refrigerator overnight so
fat hardens and can be easily removed.

Make the pie crust with 3 cups flour, 1 cup shortening, and ice water. This
should make enough for two 10-inch pies with tops. When ready to bake, pre-
heat oven to 425°. Divide crust into four balls of dough. Roll out one ball and fold
in half to slide into the pie tin and open full. Put half meat mixture into pie tin.
Now roll out another ball for the pie top. Wet edges with water, put top crust
on, and flute edges with fingers or press with a fork. Put 5 to 6 small slices in
crust top for ventilation. Repeat for second pie. Now bake at 425° for 15 minutes, turn heat down to 350° and bake for an additional 25 minutes. Serves 16.

Michigan. Although many French Canadians of the second wave resis-
ted assimilation, their children and grandchildren have joined the first
wave and are indistinct from most other Americans except for their
French surnames. The institutions they founded to protect their
descendants from assimilation no longer operate. The beneficial

societies, such as the Société St-Jean-Baptiste, no longer exist except in the Detroit area. In the 1990s, the Detroit Société had only about 100 members and was composed almost exclusively of recent immigrants from Quebec. The other chapters of the Société, as well as the other mutual benefit groups, slowly died away unnoticed after the 1930s. No French language newspaper has been published since 1957. Many French parishes are now Americanized or closed. The saddest example of this is St. Joachim, which shut its doors in 1989 thus ending 288 years of French Canadian Catholicism in Detroit.

In comparison to New England, the French Canadians of Michigan have not fared well in resisting cultural assimilation. There are several factors behind this failure. Early on, internal discord racked the French Canadian mutual benefit societies in Michigan, and they did not play as important a role in protecting French Canadian culture, as similar organizations did in New England. The Michigan French Canadians settled mostly in dispersed and isolated towns and rural areas. In New England, French Canadians concentrated in large mill towns. Most of Michigan's French Canadians never lived in crowded, multiethnic urban neighborhoods or faced stark poverty. The company towns where they lived generally provided better conditions than the tenements found in larger eastern cities. Consequently, the Michigan French Canadians did not experience the solidarity that emerged from intense conflicts with other ethnic groups as happened in New England.[36] Nor did they have to confront threats from American Know-Nothings and intolerant Yankees. In New England, reactionaries attacked French Canadians as the "Chinese of the Eastern States" and radicals viewed them as anti-labor.[37] The much milder discrimination that occurred in Michigan created no pressing need to unite to fight it. Although French Canadians across the country were among the lowest paid of the European ethnic groups in 1950, there were differences between regions. In Michigan they were economically better off than their New England counterparts due to better paying jobs in the automobile industry.[38] In sum, it was easy for Michigan's French Canadians to assimilate to the American life style.

The descendants of French Canadian immigrants now practice what Herbert Gans refers to as "symbolic ethnicity."[39] If they express their ethnicity at all, it is in ways that do not interfere with their American lifestyle. For example, the French Canadian Heritage Society of Michigan founded in 1980 to help its members conduct genealogical research is now the largest French Canadian group in Michigan with more than five hundred members. Yet, less than five percent of them can speak French fluently. It is impressive to see how many older members remember French Canadian folktales or songs at meetings with cultural presentations, but they are a dwindling proportion of the group. Younger members are further and further removed from their cultural heritage.

Despite the loss of the French language and other cultural traits, French Canadians in Michigan, young and old, use genealogy to reclaim their heritage. Genealogy has become an important pastime for many people, and it is a hobby they share with their cousins in Quebec where it is also very popular. In fact, French Canadians can boast of some of the best preserved, organized, and computerized genealogical records in the world. Many French Canadians who make trips to Quebec will combine genealogical research with visiting ancestral hometowns. Genealogy has become an important point of contact between French Canadians across North America.

Genealogical researchers have traced the lineage of the celebrity Madonna, who is one notable exception to the generalization that French Canadians avoided the limelight of fame. Michigan French Canadians share the honor with Italian Americans of giving Madonna to the musical world. Although Madonna Veronica Louise Ciccone's father was of Italian ancestry, her mother was a French Canadian Fortin from Bay City, Michigan. Her maternal great-grandparents were from Quebec. Two enterprising genealogists, one from Michigan and the other from Quebec, worked together to trace Madonna's ancestry back fourteen generations through Michigan to Quebec and then to France.[40]

Colonial history reenactment groups are another example of organizations that foster symbolic ethnicity among the French Canadians. There are several voyageur groups, *Troupes de la Marine* units for the Seven Years' period, and even a French Canadian company of the Detroit militia that served the British during the American Revolution. They hold events at sites associated with the French colonial experience including the reconstructed Fort Michilimackinac in Mackinaw

Figure 13. French colonial reenactors. Living history has become a popular way to remember the French Canadian heritage in Michigan. Courtesy of Rose and Harry Burgess.

City and Straits State Park in St. Ignace. Although their members come from a variety of ethnic backgrounds, these groups allow French Canadian participants and observers to celebrate the contribution their ancestors made to Michigan history. Despite their French colonial emphasis, very few members can speak anything more then a few awkward phrases in French.

It is ironic that while Quebec continues to debate independence, French Canadians in Michigan are politically uninvolved in this struggle. Neither the French Canadian Heritage Society of Michigan nor the Société St-Jean-Baptiste have taken an official stand on separatism. Many members of the latter group fear separatism because they believe it will damage language rights in the rest of Canada and have a negative impact on language rights in the United States. The members of the former group overwhelmingly oppose separatism because they view it as unnecessary to protect French language rights within Quebec, abusive of the language rights of English-speaking residents and visitors, harmful to the language rights of French-speakers outside of Quebec, economically unwise, and the cause of a passing minority of Quebecois.[41]

There has also been a failure to pull Michigan French Canadians together under Franco-American umbrella groups. Although the Société St-Jean-Baptiste interacts with the Alliance Française, the French Canadian Heritage Society and the reenactment groups have only haphazard and infrequent contacts with this group, which attempts to preserve French language and culture. In 1983 the Assemblée des Franco-Américains held its national congress on Mackinac Island and received some support from local Michigan groups, but it failed to leave a lasting impression or to inspire further efforts in Michigan.

For the romantic nationalist, there is something melancholy about the assimilation of the French Canadians in Michigan. But for the pragmatist—who is quintessentially American—there is something vibrant and exciting about the way the French Canadians have decided to reclaim their heritage, remember it, and display it. They do so in ways that do not interfere with their otherwise ordinary American life style.

Notes

1. W. J. Eccles, *Franco in America* (Vancouver: Fitzhenry & Whiteside Ltd., 1972), 127.

2. For the emergence of a French Canadian identity and its role in the Seven Years' War, see Guy Frégault, *Canadian Society in the French Regime* (Ottawa: The Canadian Historical Association Booklets, no. 3, 1971), 16.

3. The Acadians deserve special mention. In 1755, these French-speaking people were exiled from their homeland in Nova Scotia and New Brunswick to the American colonies, England, and France. Some of them fled to Quebec and were absorbed into the French Canadian population. An unknown number of Michigan French Canadians have Acadian ancestry through these refugees. Many other Acadians eventually returned to the Canadian Maritimes. While still other Acadians eventually migrated to Spanish-controlled Louisiana and became known as Cajuns.

4. Elliott Robert Barkan, "French Canadians," in *Harvard Encyclopedia of American Ethnic Groups* (Cambridge: Harvard University Press,1980), 389.

5. For the location of French missions in the Great Lakes, see Helen Hornbeck Tanner, ed. *Atlas of Great Lakes Indian History* (Norman: University of Oklahoma Press, 1987), 37. The mission called L'Anse was actually on the west side of Keweenaw Bay closer to Baraga, modern-day L'Anse is on the east shore of the bay.

6. Although Cadillac is viewed as a Detroit folk hero, modern scholarship has presented a less than admirable view of him. See Yves F. Zoltvany, "Laumet, dit de Lamothe Cadillac, Antoine," in *Dictionary of Canadian Biography*, comp. W. Stewart Wallace (Toronto: Macmillan, 1926), 2: 351–57.

7. Gail F. Moreau and Anita Campeau are in the process of compiling a thorough list of all the French and French Canadian settlers and pioneers of early Detroit. Their research has led to new findings about Cadillac, Madame Cadillac, and Detroit's earliest settlers. They hope to publish their findings, tentatively entitled *Those Who Came to Detroit 1701–1710*, by 2001, the tricentennial of Detroit's founding.

8. Almon Ernest Parkins, "The Historical Geography of Detroit," in *A Franco-American Overview: Midwest and West* (Cambridge, Mass.: National Assessment and Dissemination Center for Bilingual/Bicultural Education, 1980), 2: 218.

9. For an excellent history of the Fox Wars, see R. David Edmunds and Joseph L. Peyser, *The Fox Wars: The Mesquakie Challenge to New France* (Norman: University of Oklahoma Press, 1993).

10. The 1710 data are from the census found in Donna Valley Russell, ed., *Michigan Censuses 1710–1830: Under French, British, and Americans* (Detroit: Detroit Society for Genealogical Research, Inc. 1982), 4–7. The origins of these settlers were identified by using Christian Denissen, *Genealogy of the French Families of the Detroit River Region, 1701–1936*, 2 vols., 2d rev. ed. (Detroit: Detroit Society for Genealogical Research, Inc., 1987); and René Jetté, *Dictionnaire généalogique des familles du Québec* (Montréal: Les Presses de l'Université de Montréal, 1983). Only four of these settlers' origins were unidentified using these sources.

11. Independent companies of Marines or Marine troops, these colonial regulars were referred to as marines because the Ministry of Marine was responsible for the defense of New France. Michigan is an example of the militarization of New France society, due to the settlement of these soldiers at Detroit and Michililmackinac. W. J. Eccles, "The Social, Economic, and Political Significance of the Military Establishment of New France," in *Essays on New France* (Toronto: Oxford University Press, 1987), 110–24.

12. Clarence M. Burton, *The City of Detroit, Michigan, 1701–1922* (Detroit: S. J. Clarke Publishing Co., 1922), 2: 1503.

13. Ernest J. Lajeunesse, *The Windsor Border Region: Canada's Southernmost*

Frontier (Toronto: The Champlain Society and University of Toronto Press, 1960), 49-53. This list of settlers is known as the Cicotte Registry and the original is in the Burton Historical Collection. The information in Lajeunesse was compared to Denissen, *French Families*, and Jetté, *Dictionnaire généalogique*. Only two out of the twenty-seven colonists' origins were unidentified.

14. These data come from a list of Detroit commanders found in Burton, *City of Detroit*, 1: 97–113, and a posted list of commanders in the Commanding Officer's House at Colonial Fort Michililmackinac Historic Park. These data were compared with the genealogical information in Jetté, *Dictionnaire généalogique*.

15. Some of these folk tales can be found in the following publications: Richard Mercer Dorson, *Bloodstoopers & Bearwalkers: Folk Tradition of the Upper Peninsula* (Cambridge: Harvard University Press, 1952); Edith Fowke, *Folktales of·French Canada* (Toronto: NC Press, 1979); Helen Frances Gilbert, *Tonquish Tales*, 2 vols. (Plymouth, Mich.: Pilgrim Heritage Press, 1984); Dirk Gringhuis, *Were-Wolves and Will-O-The-Wisps: French Tales of Mackinac Retold* (Mackinac Island: Mackinac Island State Park Commission, 1974); and Marie Caroline Watson Hamel, *Legend of Le Détroit* (1884; reprint, Detroit: Gale Research Co., 1977). Many of the tales told in Michigan absorbed Indian elements.

16. Kerry A. Trask, "To Cast Out the Devils: British Ideology and the French Canadians of the Northwest Interior, 1760–1774," *American Review of Canadian Studies* 15, no. 3 (autumn 1985): 249–62.

17. George N. Fuller, *Michigan: A Centennial History of the State and Its People*, 5 vols. (Chicago: Lewis Publishing Co., 1939), 1:179.

18. Fuller, *Michigan*, 1:179.

19. Fuller, *Michigan*, 1:283. Willis F. Dunbar, *Michigan, A History of the Wolverine State*, rev. ed. George S. May (Grand Rapids: Eerdmans, 1980), 745.

20. Lynda Ann Ewen, *Corporate Power and Urban Crisis in Detroit* (Princeton, N.J.: Princeton University Press, 1978), 58 and chart between 77–78. She found that many Detroit ruling class families can trace back to Barthe, Campeau, DeQuindre, Moran, and Piquette ancestors.

21. Fuller, *Michigan*, 1:181.

22. Yolande Lavoie, *L'Émigration des Québécois aux États-Unis de 1840 à 1930* (Quèbec: Éditeur officiel du Québec, 1981), 52.

23. The French Canadians maintained a fertility level unmatched by most other ethnic groups in North America. It is traditionally said that this was done as a reaction to the British conquest and then continued to keep up with the growing number of non-French Canadians moving into Canada. It was popularly called the *revanche des berceaux* (revenge of the cradles). However, this traditional explanation is suspect as even during the colonial period, the French Canadians had a healthy fertility level.

24. George B. Engberg, "Who Were the Lumberjacks?" *Michigan History* 32, no. 3 (September 1948): 242.

25. Mason Wade, "French Canadians in the United States," in *Writings on Canadian-American Studies* (East Lansing: Michigan State University, 1966), 9. See also Robert Painchaud, "French Canadian Historiography and Franco-Catholic Settlement in Western Canada, 1870–1915," *Canadian Historical Review* 59, no. 4 (December 1978): 455.

26. Bruno Ramirez and Jean Lamarre, "Du Québec vers les États-Unis: L'étude des lieux d'origine," *Revue d'histoire de l'Amérique française* 38, no. 3 (winter 1985): 415–16.

27. In general, scholars have ignored the nineteenth-century French Canadians in Michigan. Several studies have been done on the French Canadians of New England, but only one scholarly study has been done on French Canadians in Michigan. This is Jean Lamarre's "La Migration des canadiens français ver le Michigan, 1840–1914: Leur contribution au développement socio-économique de la région" (Ph.D. diss., Université de Montréal, 1996). He studied the similarities and differences between French Canadian settlements on the Keweenaw Peninsula's copper range and in the Saginaw River valley's lumber area. Lamarre looked at the immigrants' strategies of adaptation in these two industrial regions. His dissertation will soon be published in French and in English.

28. U.S. Census Office, Department of Interior, *Census Reports, Population, Twelfth Census of the U.S.* (Washington, D.C., 1901), vol. 1, part 1, table 33, 732–35.

29. U.S. Bureau of the Census, Department of Commerce, *Census of Population: 1950. Characteristics of the Population. Michigan* (Washington, D.C., 1952), vol. 2, pt. 22, table 24, 22–55.

The 1990 census data show more French than French Canadians in the state. In contrast, the 1950 census indicates that French Canadians make up 81% of the Franco-Americans in the state. This discrepancy is undoubtedly due to people of French Canadian ancestry mistakenly identifying themselves as French or possibly Canadian. U.S. Bureau of the Census, Department of Commerce, *Ancestry of the Population by State: 1980 Supplementary Report* (Washington, D. C., 1983), table 4, 71. U. S. Bureau of the Census, Department of Commerce, *1990 Census of Population: Supplementary Report, Detailed Ancestry Groups for States* (No. 1990 CP-S-1-2, Washington, D.C., 1992).

30. U. S. Census Office, *Twelfth Census,* vol. 1, pt. 1, table 34, 760–61.

31. U. S. Census Office, *Twelfth Census,* vol. 1, pt. 1, table 33, 732–35.

32. *Official Catholic Directory* (New York: P. J. Kennedy & Sons, 1912), 368–78, 414–20, and 516–21.

33. For the French Canadian view see Télesphore St-Pierre, *Histoire des Canadiens du Michigan et du comté d'Essex, Ontario* (Montréal: Typographie de la Gazette, 1895), 263–66. For a more balanced view see George Paré, *The Catholic Church in Detroit, 1701–1888* (Detroit: Gabriel Richard Press, 1951), 543–47.

34. Wade, "French Canadians," 12.

35. Georges J. Joyaux, "French Press in Michigan," *Michigan History* 37, no. 2 (June 1953): 158.

36. The best example of inter-ethnic rivalry is between the French Canadians and Irish. They had different views on the issue of national parishes and often fought bitterly over it. Mason Wade credits part of this conflict to the "chosen people complex" from which both groups suffered. He also mentions that at least one French Canadian priest wondered if the two groups would be separated in heaven. Despite the intensity of their rivalry, it is ironic that many French Canadians took Irish spouses. Mason Wade, "French and French Canadians in the U.S.," *New Catholic Encyclopedia,* 6 (New York: McGraw Hill, 1967–79), 143–48.

37. Barkan, "French Canadians," 394.

38. John P. DuLong, "Avoir part au Gateau: French Canadians and Income Inequality in America," paper delivered at the French Canadian Society Session of the Association for Canadian Studies in the United States meeting, Rockport, Mass., September 1983.

39. Herbert J. Gans, "Symbolic Ethnicity: The Future of Ethnic Groups and Cultures in America," *Ethnic and Racial Studies* 2, no. 1 (January 1979): 1–20.

40. Gail F. Moreau and René Jetté, "Madonna's French Canadian Ancestry," *Michigan's Habitant Heritage* 15, no. 2 (April 1994): 39–59; 15, no. 3 (July 1994): 71–88; 15, no. 4 (October 1994): 125–36.

41. These results come from a straw vote on the independence of Quebec among approximately forty members and visitors attending a March 1991 meeting of the French Canadian Heritage Society of Michigan. Only one person in the room voted in favor of separatism.

42. Marie Gérin-Lajoie, trans. and ed., *Fort Michilimackinac in 1749: Lotbinière's Plan and Description, Mackinac History*, vol. 2, leaflet no. 5 (Mackinac Island: Mackinac Island State Park Commission, 1976), 9.

43. John F. Forster, "Life in the Copper Mines of Lake Superior," *Michigan Pioneer and Historical Collections* (Lansing: Michigan Pioneer and Historical Society, 1874–1929), 11:184.

44. See Paul Trap, "Mouet de Langlade, Charles,-Michael," in *Dictionary of Canadian Biography*, 4:563–64; and Keith R. Widder, *Battle for the Soul: Métis Children Encounter Evangelical Protestants at Mackinaw Mission, 1823–1837* (East Lansing: Michigan State University Press, 1999), 50–54.

For Further Reference

Reenactment Organizations

- *Compagnie franche de la Marine du Detroit de Muy*, c/o Donald F. Shaffer, 7243 Shaffer Road, Belleville, OH 44813; *http://www.richnet.net/~kamoore*
- *La Detachement, La Milice du Détroit*, c/o Andrew Gallup, 265 E. Wood St., Shreve, OH 44676; *http://members.aol.com/Dyg46/index.html*
- *La Compagnie de Jean-Baptiste Campeau de la Milice de Détroit*, c/o Patricia Greim, Monroe County Historical Commission, 126 S. Monroe St., Monroe, MI 48161

Genealogical Organizations

- Detroit Society for Genealogical Research, Inc., c/o Burton Historical Collection, Detroit Public Library, 5201 Woodward Ave., Detroit, MI 48202; *http://www.dsgr.org*
- Detroit Chapter of the French-Canadian Heritage Society of Michigan, c/o The Burton Historical Collection, Detroit Public Library, 5201 Woodward Ave., Detroit, MI 48202
- Essex Branch of the Ontario Genealogical Society, P.O. Box 2, Station "A", Windsor, ON N9A 6J5; *http://www.rootsweb.com/~onsxogs/ogs1.htm*
- French Canadian Heritage Society of Michigan, P.O. Box 10028, Lansing, MI 48901-0028; *http://habitant.org/fchsm*

- French Colonial Heritage Society (Host society for *Les soldats de la troupes de la marines de la compagnie du Belêtre*), c/o Port Huron Museum, 1115 Sixth St., Port Huron, MI 48060-5346
- Genealogical Society of Monroe County, P.O. Box 1428, Monroe, MI 48161-6428; *http://www.tdi.net/havekost/gsmc.htm*
- *Société franco-ontarienne d'histoire et de généalogie*, Windsor-Essex Branch, C.P. 1021, rue Meunier, Belle Rivière, ON N0R 1A0; Tel. (519) 728-4742. (Research Center at the Community Center of St-Simon-St-Jude Church. Excellent library containing much valuable information relating to French Canadian families in both Ontario and Michigan.)

Museums

- Bay County Historical Museum, 321 Washington, Bay City, MI 48708-5837; Tel. (517) 893-5733
- The Detroit Historical Museum, 5401 Woodward Ave. (at Kirby), Detroit, MI 48202; Tel. (313) 833-1805; *http://www.detroithistorical.org*
- Father Marquette National Memorial and Museum, St. Ignace, MI 49781; Tel. (906) 643-9394; *http://sos.state.mi.us/history/museum/musemarg*
- Fort St. Joseph Museum, 508 Main St., Niles, MI 49120; Tel. (616) 683-4702; *http://www.ci.niles.mi.us/Living/Museum.htm*
- Hartwick Pines Lumbering Museum, Route 3, Box 3840, Grayling, MI 49738; Tel. (517) 348-7068; *http://sos.state.mi.us/history/museum/musehart*
- Houghton County Historical Museum, 5500 Highway M-26, P.O. Box 127, Lake Linden, MI 49945; Tel. (906) 296-4121; *http://habitant.org/houghton*
- Keweenaw National Historical Park, P.O. Box 471, Calumet, MI 49931; Tel. (800) 338-7982, Keweenaw Tourism Council; Tel. (906) 337-3168, Park Office; *http://www.nps.gov/kewe*
- Mackinac State Historic Parks (Consisting of Colonial Michilimackinac, Historic Mill Creek, Fort Mackinac, and Mackinac Island State Park), P.O. Box 370, Mackinac Island, MI 49757; Tel. (906) 847-3328, summer, (616) 436-4100 or (517) 373-4296 winter; *http://www.mackinac.com/historicparks*
- Marquette County Historical Society (Offers a museum and the J. M. Longyear Research Library), 213 N. Front St., Marquette, MI 49855-4292; Tel. (906) 226-3571
- Michigan Historical Museum, Michigan Library and Historical Center, 717 W. Allegan, Lansing, MI 48918; Tel. (517) 373-3559; *http://sos.state.mi.us/history/museum/explore/museums/hismus/hismus.html*

- Michigan Iron Industry Museum, 73 Forge Road, Negaunee, MI 49866; Tel. (906) 475-7857; *http://sos.state.mi.us/history/museum/museiron.html*
- Michigan State University Museum, West Circle Drive, Lansing, MI 48824-1045; Tel. (517) 355-2370; *http://museum.msu.edu*
- Monroe County Historical Commission, 126 S. Monroe St., Monroe, MI 48161; Tel. (734) 243-7137; *http://monroe.lib.mi.us/cwis/mchc.htm*
- Saginaw County Historical Museum, 500 Federal St., Saginaw, MI 48607-1253; Tel. (517) 752-2861

Libraries and Archives

- Burton Historical Collection, Detroit Public Library, 5201 Woodward Ave., Detroit, MI 48202; Tel. (313) 833-1480
- Copper Country Historical Collections, J. R. Van Pelt Library, Michigan Technological University, 1400 Townsend Drive, Houghton, MI 49931-1295; Tel. (906) 487-3209; Fax (906) 487-2357; *http://www.lib.mtu.edu/jrvp/mtuarchives/mtuarchives.htm*
- Hoyt Public Library, 505 Janes St., Saginaw, MI 48607; Tel. (517) 755-0904; Fax (517) 755-9829; *http://saginaw.lib.mi.us/Branches/Hoyt_Main_Library/hoyt_main_library.html*
- Library of Michigan, Genealogy and Local History Collection, Michigan Library and Historical Center, 717 W. Allegan St., P.O. Box 30007, Lansing, MI 48909; Tel. (517) 373-1300; *http://www.libofmich.lib.mi.us*
- State Archives of Michigan, Michigan Library and Historical Center, 717 W. Allegan St., Lansing, MI 48918-1837; Tel. (517) 373-1408; *http://www.sos.state.mi.us/history/archive/archive.html*

Music

- *12 Voyageur Songs*. Artists: Male Choir of the Université de Moncton, New Brunswick. Minnesota Historical Society, Order Department, 1500 Mississippi St., St. Paul, MN 55101, no. C-30, n. d.
- *Un Canadien errant: French Music in the North American Tradition*. Artists: Lilian Labbé and Don Hinkley. Philo Records, distributed by Rounder Records, One Camp St., Cambridge, MA 02140, Philo no. C-PH-1069, 1987.
- *Vieilles chansons du Détroit: Old French Songs of the Detroit River Region*. Artist: Marcel Bénéteau. Essex County Historical Society, c/o 254 Pitt West, Windsor, ON N9A 5L5, no. ECHS 1, 1992.
- *Vieilles chansons du Détroit: Old French Songs of the Detroit River Region*,

Vol. 2. Artist: Marcel Bénéteau. Disques Petite Côte Records, Marcel Bénéteau, 247 Esdras Place, Windsor, ON N8S 2M4 (519) 945-7652, no. PC001, 1995.

Printed Sources

Armour, David A., and Keith R. Widder. *At the Crossroads: Michilimackinac During the American Revolution.* Mackinac Island: Mackinac Island State Park Commission, 1986.

Au, Dennis. "Marie Thérèse Lasselle." *Michigan History* 76, no. 4 (July/August 1992): 13–17.

Au, Dennis M., and Joanna Brode. "The Lingering Shadow of New France: The French-Canadian Community of Monroe County, Michigan." In *Michigan Folklife Reader,* edited by C. Kurt Dewhurst and Yvonne Lockwood. East Lansing: Michigan State University Press, 1987.

Balesi, Charles J. *The Time of the French in the Heart of North America, 1673–1818.* Chicago: Alliance Française, 1992.

Barkan, Elliott Robert. "French Canadians." In *The Harvard Encyclopedia of American Ethnic Groups,* edited by Stephan Thernstrom. Cambridge, Mass.: Harvard University. Press, 1980.

Beck, Earl Clifton. *Songs of the Michigan Lumberjack.* Ann Arbor: University of Michigan Press, 1941.

———. *Lore of the Lumber Camps.* Ann Arbor: University of Michigan Press, 1948.

Bidlack, Russell E. *The Yankee Meets the Frenchman: River Raisin 1817–1830.* Ann Arbor: Historical Society of Michigan, Occasional Publications Series, 1965.

Briggs, Winstanley. "Le Pays des Illinois." *William and Mary Quarterly,* 3d ser., 47, no. 1 (January 1990): 30–56.

Brown, Donald Andrew. "Socio-Cultural Development and Archaeological Cultural patterning on the Lower Great Lakes Frontiers of New France." Ph.D. diss., University of Toronto, 1985.

Brown, Henry D., Henri Négrié, Frank R. Place, René Toujas, Leonard N. Simons, Solan Weeks, and others. *Cadillac and the Founding of Detroit: Commemorating the Two Hundred and Seventy-fifth Anniversary of the Founding of the City of Detroit by Antoine Laumet de Lamothe Cadillac on July 24, 1701.* Detroit: Detroit Historical Society and Wayne State University Press, 1976.

Burton, Clarence M. *The City of Detroit, Michigan, 1701–1922.* 5 vols. Detroit: S. J. Clarke Publishing Co., 1922.

———. *Cadillac's Village: Detroit Under Cadillac with List of Property Owners and a History of the Settlement, 1701–1710.* Detroit: Detroit Society for Genealogical Research, Inc., 1999.

Chaput, Donald. "Le Courrier du Michigan." *Historical Society of Michigan Chronicle* 4, no. 8 (December 1968): 3–5.

———. "Some Repatriement Dilemmas." *Canadian Historical Review* 49, no. 4 (December 1968): 400–12.

Chouquette, Leslie. *Frenchmen into Peasants: Modernity and Tradition in the Peopling of French Canada.* Cambridge, Mass.: Harvard University Press, 1997.

Denissen, Christian. *Genealogy of the French Families of the Detroit River Region, 1701–1936.* 2d rev. ed., 2 vols. Detroit: Detroit Society for Genealogical Research, Inc, 1987.

Dictionary of Canadian Biography. 14 vols. to date. Toronto: University of Toronto Press, 1966–.

Dorson, Richard Mercer. *Bloodstoopers & Bearwalkers: Folk Tradition of the Upper Peninsula.* Cambridge, Mass.: Harvard University Press, 1952.

DuLong, John P. "Avoir part au Gateau: French-Canadians and Income Inequality in America." Paper delivered at the French Canadian Society Session of the Association for Canadian Studies in the United States meeting, Rockport, Maine, 30 September 1983.

———. "French Canadian Genealogical Research in Houghton County, Michigan." *Michigan's Habitant Heritage,* 5 part series, 10, no. 4 (October 1989): 98–103; 11, no. 1 (January 1990): 19–21; 11, no. 2 (April 1990): 39–44; 11, no. 3 (July 1990): 56–59; and 11, no. 4 (October 1990): 82–86.

Dunbar, Willis F. *Michigan: A History of the Wolverine State.* Rev. ed. Edited by George S. May. Grand Rapids: William B. Eerdmans Publishing Co., 1980.

Eccles, W. J. *The Canadian Frontier, 1534–1760.* Rev. ed. Albuquerque: University. of New Mexico Press, 1983.

———. *The French in North America, 1500–1783.* East Lansing: Michigan State University Press, 1998.

———. "The Social, Economic, and Political Significance of the Military Establishment of New France." In *Essays on New France.* Toronto: Oxford University Press, 1987.

Edmunds, R. David. "'Unacquainted with the Laws of the Civilized World': American Attitudes toward the Métis Communities in the Old Northwest." In *The New Peoples: Being and Becoming Métis in North America*, edited by Jacquelyn Peterson and Jennifer S. H. Brown. Winnipeg: University of Manitoba Press, 1985.

Edmunds, R. David, and Joseph L. Peyser. *The Fox Wars: The Mesquakie Challenge to New France*. Norman: University of Oklahoma Press, 1993.

Engberg, George B. "Who Were the Lumberjacks?" *Michigan History* 32, no. 3 (September 1948): 238–46.

Farmer, Silas. *History of Detroit and Wayne County and Early Michigan: A Chronological Cyclopedia of the Past and Present*. 3d ed., rev. and enl. Detroit, Gale Research Co., 1969.

Ford, Richard Clyde. "The French-Canadians in Michigan." *Michigan History* 27, no. 2 (spring 1943): 243–57.

Forster, John H. "Life in the Copper Mines of Lake Superior." *Michigan Pioneer and Historical Collections*, 11 (1887): 175–186.

Fowke, Edith. *Folktales of French Canada*. Toronto: NC Press Ltd., 1979.

Frégault, Guy. *Canadian Society in the French Regime*. Ottawa: The Canadian Historical Association Booklets, no. 3, 1971.

Fuller, George N. *Michigan: A Centennial History of the State and Its People*. 5 vols. Chicago: Lewis Publishing Co., 1939.

Gans, Herbert J. "Symbolic Ethnicity: The Future of Ethnic Groups and Cultures in America." *Ethnic and Racial Studies* 2, no. 1 (January 1979): 1–20.

Genser, Wallace. "'Habitants,' 'Half-Breeds,' and Homeless Children: Transformations in Métis and Yankee-Yorker Relations in Early Michigan." *Michigan Historical Review* 24, no. 1 (spring 1998): 23–47.

Gérin-Lajoie, Marie, ed. and trans. "Fort Michilimackinac in 1749: Lotbinière's Plan and Description." *Mackinac History*. Vol. 2, leaflet no. 5. Mackinac Island: Mackinac Island State Park Commission, 1976.

Gilbert, Helen Frances. *Tonquish Tales*. 2 vols. Plymouth, Mich.: Pilgrim Heritage Press, 1984.

Graff, George P. "French and French Canadians—Our Earliest Immigrants." In *The People of Michigan*. 2d rev. ed. Lansing: Michigan Department of Education, State Library Services, 1974.

Gringhuis, Dirk. *Were-Wolves and Will-O-The-Wisps: French Tales of Mackinac Retold*. Mackinac Island: Mackinac Island State Park Commission, 1974.

Hamil, Fred Coyne. "The French Heritage of the Detroit Region." *Michigan History* 47, no. 1 (March 1963): 41–46.

Hamil, Marie Caroline Watson. *Legends of Le Détroit.* 1884; reprint, Detroit: Gale Research Co., 1977.

Harris, R. Cole, R. Louis Gentilcore, and Donald Kerr, eds. *Historical Atlas of Canada.* 3 vols. Toronto: University of Toronto Press, 1987–1993

Holli, Melvin G. "French Detroit: The Clash of Feudal and Yankee Values." In *The Ethnic Frontier: Essays in the History of Group Survival in Chicago and the Midwest.* Grand Rapids: William B. Eerdmans Publishing Co., 1977.

Hubbard, Bela. *Memorials of a Half-Century in Michigan and the Lake Region.* 1888; Detroit: Gale Research Co., 1978.

Jarvis, Brad Devin Edward. "A 'Woman Much to be Respected': Madeline Laframboise and the Redefinition of a Métis Identity." Master's thesis, Michigan State University, 1998.

Jetté, René, *Dictionnaire généalogique des familles du Québec.* Montréal: Les Presses de l'Université de Montréal, 1983

Joyaux, Georges J. "French Press in Michigan: A Bibliography." Michigan History 36, no. 3 (September 1952): 260–78.

———. "French Press in Michigan." *Michigan History* 37, no. 2 (June 1953): 155–65.

Karamanski, Theodore J. *Deep Woods Frontier: A History of Logging in Northern Michigan.* Detroit: Wayne State University Press, 1989.

Kilar, Jeremy W. *Michigan's Lumbertowns: Lumbermen and Laborers in Saginaw, Bay City, and Muskegon, 1870–1905.* Detroit: Wayne State University Press, 1990.

Lajeunesse, Ernest J. *The Windsor Border Region: Canada's Southernmost Frontier.* Toronto: Champlain Society, University of Toronto Press, 1960.

Lamarre, Jean. "La Migration des canadiens français ver le Michigan, 1840–1914: Leur contribution au développement socio-économique de la région." Ph.D. diss., Université de Montréal, 1996.

———. "Migration Patterns and Socio-Economic Intergration of the French Canadians in the Saginaw Valley, Michigan, 1840–1900." *Mid-America: An Historical Review* 80, no. 3 (autumn 1998): 117–208.

Lavoie, Yolande. *L'Émigration des Québécois aux États-Unis de 1840 à 1930.* Québec: Éditeur officiel du Québec, 1981.

Maybee, Rolland H. *Michigan's White Pine Era, 1840–1900.* Lansing: Michigan Historical Commission, 1960.

McQuillan, D. Aidan. "French-Canadian Communities in the American Upper Midwest During the Nineteenth Century." *Cahiers de Géographie du Québec* 23, no. 58 (April 1979): 53–72.

Mills, James Cooke. *History of Saginaw County.* 2 vols. Saginaw, Mich.: Seemann & Peters, 1918.

Monette, Clarence J. *Gregoryville: The History of a Hamlet Located Across from Lake Linden, Michigan.* Lake Linden: By the Author, 1974.

Moogk, Peter. *La Nouvelle France: The Making of French Canada—A Cultural History.* East Lansing: Michigan State University Press, 2000.

Moreau, Gail F., and Anita Campeau. *Those Who Came to Detroit 1701–1710.* Forthcoming.

Moreau, Gail F., and René Jetté. "Madonna's French-Canadian Ancestry." *Michigan's Habitant Heritage* 15, no. 2 (April 1994): 39–59; 15, no. 3 (July 1994): 71–88; 15, no. 4 (October 1994):125–36.

Myers, Robert C., and Joseph L. Peyser. "Four Flags over Fort St. Joseph." *Michigan History* 75, no. 5 (September/October 1991): 11–21.

Nute, Grace Lee. *The Voyageur.* St. Paul, Minn.: Minnesota Historical Society, 1955.

Official Catholic Directory. New York: P. J. Kennedy & Sons, Publishers, 1912.

Old French Town Cookery: Including Receipts from the Cookbooks of Descendants of French Residents of Monroe County, Michigan. Monroe: Monroe County Historical Society, 1979.

Painchaud, Robert. "French-Canadian Historiography and Franco-Catholic Settlement in Western Canada, 1870–1915." *Canadian Historical Review* 59, no. 4 (December 1978): 447–66.

Paré, George. *The Catholic Church in Detroit, 1701–1888.* Detroit: Gabriel Richard Press, 1951.

Parker, James Hill. *Ethnic Identity: The Case of the French Americans.* Washington, DC: University Press of America, 1983.

Parkins, Almon Ernest. "The Historical Geography of Detroit." In *A Franco-American Overview: Midwest and West.* Cambridge, Mass.: National Assessment and Dissemination Center for Bilingual/Bicultural Education, 1980.

Peckham, Howard H. *Pontiac and the Indian Uprising.* 1947; Reprint, Detroit: Wayne State University Press, 1994 .

Petersen, Eugene T. *France at Mackinac: A Pictorial Record of French Life and Culture, 1715–1760.* Mackinac Island: Mackinac Island State Park Commission, 1968.

Peterson, Jacqueline. "Prelude to Red River: A Social Portrait of the Great Lakes Métis." *Ethnohistory* 25, no. 1 (winter 1978): 41– 67.

———. "The People in Between: Indian-White Marriage and the Genesis of a Metis Society and Culture in the Great Lakes Region, 1680–1830." Ph.D. diss., University of Illinois at Chicago, 1981.

Peyser, Joseph L. *Jacques Legardeur de Saint-Pierre: Officer, Gentleman, Entrepreneur.* East Lansing: Michigan State University Press, and Mackinac Island: Mackinac State Historic Parks, 1996.

———. *Letters from New France: The Upper Country, 1686–1783.* Urbana: University of Illinois Press, 1992.

Quinlan, Maria. "Lumbering in Michigan." *Great Lakes Informant.* Michigan Department of State, Michigan History Division, pamphlet, ser. 1, no., 6, 1975, 4 pages.

Ramirez, Bruno. *On the Move: French-Canadians and Italian Migrants in the North Atlantic Economy, 1860–1914.* Toronto: McClelland & Stewart, Inc., 1991.

Ramirez, Bruno, and Jean Lamarre. "Du Québec vers les États-Unis: L'étude des lieux d'origine." *Revue d'histoire de l'Amérique française* 38, no. 3 (winter 1985): 409–22.

Russell, Donna Valley, ed. *Michigan Censuses 1710–1830: Under French, British, and Americans.* Detroit: Detroit Society for Genealogical Research, Inc., 1982.

Schenck, Theresa. "The Cadots: The First Family of Sault Ste. Marie." *Michigan History* 72, no. 2 (March–April 1988): 36–43.

———. "The Cadottes: Five Generations of Fur Traders on Lake Superior." In *The Fur Trade Revisited: Selected Papers of the Sixth North American Fur Trade Conference, Mackinac Island, Michigan, 1991,* edited by Jennifer S. H. Brown, W. J. Eccles, and Donald P. Heldman, 189–98. East Lansing: Michigan State University Press, 1994.

Scott, Elizabeth M. *Archaeological Completion Report Series, No. 9., French Subsistence at Fort Michilimackinac 1715–1781: The Clergy and the Traders.* Mackinac Island: Mackinac Island State Park Commission, 1985.

Sleeper-Smith, Susan. "Silent Tongues, Black Robes: Potawatomi, Europeans, and Settlers in the Southern Great Lakes, 1640–1850." Ph.D. diss., University of Michigan, 1994.

———. "Furs and Female Kin Network: The World of Marie Madeleine Réaume

L'archevêque Chevalier." In *New Faces of the Fur Trade: Selected Papers of the Seventh North American Fur Trade Conference, Halifax, Nova Scotia, 1995*, edited by Jo-Anne Fiske, Susan Sleeper-Smith, and William Wickens, 53-72. East Lansing: Michigan State University Press, 1998.

St-Pierre, Télesphore. *Histoire des Canadiens du Michigan et du comté d'Essex, Ontario*. Montréal: Typographie de la Gazette, 1895.

Stone, Lyle M. *Fort Michilimackinac 1715–1781: An Archaeological Perspective on the Revolutionary Frontier.* East Lansing: The Museum, Michigan State University, 1974.

Tanner, Helen Hornbeck, ed. *Atlas of Great Lakes Indian History.* Norman, Okla.: University of Oklahoma Press, 1987.

———. *Strangers and Sojourners: A History of Michigan's Keweenaw Peninsula.* Detroit: Wayne State University Press, 1994.

Trap, Paul. "Mouet de Langlade, Charles-Michel." In *Dictionary of Canadian Biography*, 4:563–64, 1979.

Trask, Kerry A. "To Cast Out the Devils: British Ideology and the French Canadians of the Northwest Interior, 1760–1774." *American Review of Canadian Studies* 15, no. 3 (autumn 1985): 249-62.

———. "Settlement in a Half-Savage Land: Life and Loss in the Métis Community of La Baye." *Michigan Historical Review* 15, no. 1 (spring 1989): 1–27.

U.S. Bureau of the Census, Department of Commerce. *Census of Population: 1950. Characteristics of the Population.* Michigan. Vol. 2, pt. 22, table 24, 22–55. Washington, D.C., 1952.

———. *Ancestry of the Population by State: 1980.* Supplementary Report. Washington, D.C., 1983.

———. *1990 Census of Population: Supplementary Reports, Detailed Ancestry Groups for States.* No. 1990 CP-S-1-2. Washington, D.C., 1992.

U.S. Census Office, Department of Interior. *Census Reports, Population, Twelfth Census of the U.S.* Vol. 1, pt. 1, table 33, 732–735, and table 34, 760–761. Washington, D.C., 1901.

———. *Special Reports: Occupations at the Twelfth Census.* Table 41, 306–311. Washington, D.C., 1904.

Vander Hill, C. Warren. *Settling the Great Lakes Frontier: Immigration to Michigan, 1837–1924.* Lansing: Michigan Historical Commission, 1970.

Voelker, Donald W. "Joseph Campau: Detroit's 'Big Shot'." *Michigan History* 75, no. 4 (July/August 1991): 39–43.

Wade, Mason. "French Canadians in the United States." In *Writings on Canadian-American Studies*. East Lansing: Committee on Canadian-American Studies, Michigan State University, 1966.

———. "French and French-Canadians in the U.S." In *New Catholic Encyclopedia*, 1967.

Walthall, John A. *French Colonial Archaeology: The Illinois Country and the Western Great Lakes*. Urbana: University of Illinois Press, 1991.

Walthall, John A., and Thomas E. Emerson. *Calumet & Fleur-de-lys: Archaeology of Indian and French Contact in the Midcontinent*. Washington, D.C.: Smithsonian Institution Press, 1992.

White, Richard. *The Middle Ground: Indians, Empires, and Republics in the Great Lakes Region, 1650–1815*. Cambridge: Cambridge University Press, 1991.

Widder, Keith R. *Battle for the Soul: Métis Children Encounter Evangelical Protestants at Mackinaw Mission, 1823–1837*. East Lansing: Michigan State University Press, 1999.

Zoltvany, Yves F. "Laument, dit de Lamothe Cadillac, Antoine." In *Dictionary of Canadian Biography*, 2: 351–57, 1982.

Index